SHEDDING LIGHT ON THE POSSIBILITY OF SEEING PROPHETS AND ANGELS

Shedding Light on the Possibility of Seeing Prophets and Angels

Tanwīr al-Ḥalak fī Imkān Ru'yah al-Nabī wa al-Malak

by Imam Jalāl al-Dīn al-Suyūṭī

Translated by
Talut ibn Sulaiman Dawood

Title: Shedding Light on the Possibility of Seeing Prophets and Angels
ISBN: 978-1-952306-02-0
First Edition– April 2020

Author: Imam Jalāl al-Dīn al-Suyūṭī
Translator: Talut ibn Sulaiman Dawood
Typesetter: Imran Rahim ◆ enquiries@ethereadesign.com
Proofreader & Editor: Wordsmiths ◆ wordsmiths.org.uk ◆ info@wordsmiths.org.uk

Imam Ghazali
INSTITUTE

Contents

Biography of al-Suyūṭī

(b. 849 h. – d. 911 in Cairo)

BY DR. G. F. HADDAD

ʿAbd al-Raḥmān ibn Kamāl al-Dīn Abī Bakr ibn Muḥammad ibn Sābiq al-Dīn Jalāl al-Dīn al-Misrī al-Suyūṭī al-Shāfiʿī al-Ashʿarī (849-911), also known as Ibn al-Suyūṭī, was a *mujtahid* imam and reformer of the tenth Islamic century. He was a prominent Hadith Master, jurist, Sufi, philologist and historian, who authored works in virtually every Islamic science.

Born to a Turkish mother and a father of Persian origin, he was raised as an orphan in Cairo. He memorized the Qur'an at the age of eight, followed by several complete works of Sacred Law, fundamentals of jurisprudence, and Arabic grammar. He then devoted his life to studying the Sacred Sciences under approximately 150 sheikhs. Among them were the foremost Shāfiʿī and Ḥanafī sheikhs at the time, such as Sheikh al-Islām Sirāj al-Dīn al-Bulqīnī, with whom he studied Shāfiʿī jurisprudence; the Hadith scholar Sheikh al-Islām Sharāf al-Dīn al-Munāwī, with whom he read Qur'anic exegesis and who commented on al-Suyūṭī's *Al-jāmiʿ al-ṣaghīr* in a book entitled *Fayḍ al-Qadīr*; and Taqī al-Dīn al-Shamani, with whom he studied Hadith and the sciences of Arabic. Al-Suyūṭī also studied with Jalāl al-Dīn al-Maḥallī, a specialist in the principles of the law, together with whom he compiled the most widespread, condensed commentary on the Qur'an of our time: *Tafsīr al-Jalālayn*. Some Ḥanafī sheikhs he studied under include Shihāb al-Dīn al-Sharmisahi, Muḥyī al-Dīn al-Kafayjī, and the Hadith Master Sayf al-Dīn Qāsim ibn Qaṭlūbaghā.

In the pursuit of knowledge, al-Suyūṭī travelled to Damascus, the Hejaz, Yemen, India and Morocco, as well as to centers of learning in Egypt such as Maḥalla, Dumyāṭ, and Fayyūm. He spent some time as the head teacher of Hadith at the Shaykhuniyya school in Cairo, at the recommendation of Imam Kamāl al-Dīn ibn al-Humām. He then took up the same position at Baybarsiyya, but was dismissed due to complaints from other sheikhs whom he had replaced. After this, he retired into scholarly seclusion and did not return to the field of teaching.

Ibn Iyās, in *Tārīkh Miṣr,* reveals that when al-Suyūṭī reached forty years of age, he abandoned the company of men for the solitude of the garden of *al-Miqyās*, by the side of the river Nile, where he avoided his former colleagues as though he had never known them. It was there that he authored the majority of his nearly 600 books and treatises. Wealthy Muslims and princes would visit him with offers of money and gifts but he rejected them and also refused the Sultan many times when he requested al-Suyūṭī s presence. He once said to the Sultan's envoy: 'Do not ever come back to us with a gift, for in truth Allah has put an end to all such needs for us.'

He was blessed with great success in his years of solitude making it difficult to name a field in which al-Suyūṭī did not make outstanding contributions. Among his most prominent works is his ten-volume Hadith collection *Jamᶜ al-Jawāmiᶜ* ('The Collection of Collections'); his Qur'anic exegesis *Tafsīr al-Jalālayn* ('Commentary of the Two Jalāls') in which he finished the second half of an uncompleted manuscript by Jalāl al-Dīn Maḥallī in just forty days; and his classic commentary on the sciences of Hadith *Tadrīb al-Rāwī fi Sharḥ Taqrīb al-Nawawī* ('The Training of the Hadith Transmitter: An Exegesis of Nawawī's "The Facilitation"').

A giant among contemporary scholars, he produced a sustained output of scholarly writings until his death at the age of sixty two. He was buried in *Hawsh Qawsūn* in Cairo. In the introduction to his book entitled *al-Riyāḍ al-Anīqa* on the names of the Prophet ﷺ he said: 'It is my hope that Allah accepts this book and that through this book I shall gain the intercession of the Prophet ﷺ. Perhaps it shall be that Allah makes it the seal of all my works, and grants me what I have asked Him with longing, regarding the Honorable One.'

The editors of *Dalīl Makhṭūṭāt al-Suyūṭī* ('Guide to al-Suyūṭī's Manuscripts') have listed 723 works to his name.[1] Some of these are brief fatwas which do not exceed four pages, such as his notes on the hadith

'Whoever says: "I am knowledgeable" he is ignorant' entitled *Aᶜdhab al-Manāhil fī Hadith Man Qāla Ana ᶜĀlim*. Other works of his, for instance *Itqān fī ᶜUlūm al-Qur'ān* and *Tadrīb al-Rāwī*, are complete tomes.

Al-Ṭabarānī stated that the above hadith is only narrated through the chain containing al-Layth ibn Abī Sulaym, which is a weak chain. Al-ᶜAjlūnī in *Kashf al-Khafā'* says that this hadith is narrated by al-Ṭabarānī in *al-Awsaṭ* from Ibn ᶜUmar, rather than the Prophet ﷺ. Al-Haytamī states in *al-Fatāwa al-Hadithīyya* that this is simply a saying of the tābi'ī Yaḥyā ibn Kathīr. For his part, Ibn Kathīr cites it from ᶜUmar in his *tafsīr* of the verse: *'Have you not seen those who praise themselves for purity?'* (*al-Nisā'* 4: 49).Three narrations regarding this hadith are mentioned from ᶜUmar in *Kanz al-ᶜUmmāl*, but all of them are weak.

Al-ᶜIrāqī in his *al-Mughnī* explains that the part actually attributed to Yaḥyā ibn Kathīr is: 'Whoever says: "I am a believer", he is a disbeliever' while al-Haythamī in *Majmaᶜ al-Zawā'id* cites from Ibn Kathīr, with a weak chain, as follows: 'Whoever says: "I am knowledgeable", he is ignorant, and whoever says: "I am ignorant", he is ignorant. Whoever says: "I am in Paradise", he is in the Fire, and whoever says: "I am in the Fire", he is in the Fire.' Al-Haythamī further added: 'It is established from countless Companions and others that they said they were knowledgeable, and they would not do anything which the Prophet ﷺ had criticized. A greater proof is Yusuf's statement: "I am a knowledgeable guardian"' (*Yūsuf* 12: 55).

However, the narration of al-Layth is confirmed by the hadith of the Prophet ﷺ:

> Islam shall be on the rise until traders take to the sea [carrying it], and horses charge in the cause of Allah. After that, a people will come and recite the Qur'an, saying: 'Who recites it better than us? Who is more knowledgeable than us? Who is wiser than us?' Then he turned to his Companions and asked: 'Is there any good in such as these?' They said: 'Allah and His Prophet know best.' He said: 'Those are from among you, O *ummah*! Those are fodder for the Fire.'[2]

A reconciling factor is that the hadith of Ibn Abī Sulaym applies to those who claim knowledge either undeservedly or proudly, and not to those who act out of sincerity and obligation. Ibn ᶜAṭā' Allāh said in his *Ḥikam*:

> The root of every disobedience, forgetfulness, and desire is contentment with the self, while the root of every obedience, vigilance, and continence is your dissatisfaction with it. That you accompany an ignorant who is not pleased with himself is better for you than to accompany a knowledgeable person who is pleased with himself. And what ignorance is that of one who is dissatisfied with himself? And what knowledge is that of one who is satisfied with himself?

Imam al-Shaʿrānī in *al-ʿUhud al-Muḥammadīyya* ('The Pledges We Made to the Prophet ﷺ') made a similar statement:

> The Prophet ﷺ took our pledge that we should not claim to possess knowledge except for a licit cause, and that we should never say: 'We are the most knowledgeable of people' neither with our mouths nor with our hearts. How could we say such a thing when we know full well that in our country, let alone our region, there is one who is more knowledgeable than we? But if it is one day ordained for us to claim knowledge, then we must immediately follow this with repentance and ask forgiveness, lest punishment descend on us. This is a problem which no wise person ever faces, for there is no science which one has looked up, except the scholars of knowledge anticipated him and wrote books about it, scholars whose pupil he may not even deserve to be.

Al-Suyūṭī's student and biographer Shams al-Dīn al-Dāwūdī al-Mālikī, the author of *Ṭabaqāt al-Mufassirīn al-Kubrā*, said: 'I saw the sheikh with my own eyes writing and finishing three works in one day which he himself authored and proofread. At the same time, he was dictating hadith and replying beautifully to whatever was brought to his attention.' Al-Sakhāwī reproached him for his plagiarism of earlier books, and others added that the profusion of his works were the reason they were often incomplete, and for the frequency of flaws and contradictions in them. This is a charge commonly laid at the door of prolific authors, such as Ibn al-Jawzī and Ibn Taymīyyah. Also note that there was some animosity between al-Suyūṭī and his sheikh, al-Sakhāwī, as exhibited in the former's tract *al-Kāwī fī al-Radd ʿalā al-Sakhāwī* ('The Searing Brand in Refuting al-Sakhāwī') and his unflattering mention in the poem *Nazm al-'Iqyān fī Aʿyān al-Aʿyān.*

His chain of transmission in *taṣawwuf* goes back to Sheikh ᶜAbd al-Qādir al-Jilānī. Al-Suyūṭī belonged to the Shādhili *ṭarīqa*, which he eulogized in his brief defence of *taṣawwuf* entitled *Tashyīd al-Haqīqa al-ᶜAliyya*. In the book, he states: 'I have looked at the matters which the Imams of Shariah have criticized in Sufis, and I did not see a single true Sufi holding such positions. Rather, they are held by the people of innovation and the extremists who have claimed for themselves the title of Sufi while in reality they are not.' In the *Tashyīd* he also produces narrative chains of transmission proving that al-Ḥasan al-Baṣrī did in fact narrate directly from ᶜAlī ibn Abī Ṭālib (*raḍiyallāhu ᶜanhu*). This goes against the commonly received opinion among the scholars of hadith[3] although it was also the opinion of Imam Aḥmad ibn Ḥanbal.[4]

When one of his sheikhs, Burhān al-Dīn Ibrāhīm ibn ᶜUmar al-Biqāᶜī (d. 885), attacked Ibn ᶜArabī in a tract entitled *Tanbīh al-Ghabī ilā Takfīr Ibn ᶜArabī* ('Warning to the Dolt That Ibn ᶜArabī is an Apostate'), al-Suyūṭī countered with a tract entitled *Tanbīh Al-Ghabī fī Takhṭi'a Ibn ᶜArabī* ('Warning to the Dolt That Faults Ibn ᶜArabī'). Both epistles have been published.[5] In his reply, al-Suyūṭī states that he considers Ibn ᶜArabī a Friend of Allah whose writings are forbidden to those who read them without first learning the technical terms used by the Sufis. He cites from Ibn Ḥajar's list in *Anbā' al-Ghumr*, the trusted scholars who kept a good opinion of Ibn ᶜArabī or counted him a *walī*: Ibn ᶜAṭā' Allāh al-Iskandarī (d. 709), al-Yāfiᶜī (d. 678), Ibn ᶜAbd al-Salām after the latter's meeting with al-Shādhilī, Shihāb al-Dīn Abū al-ᶜAbbās Aḥmad ibn Yaḥyā al-Malwī al-Tilimsānī (d. 776), Sirāj al-Dīn Abū Ḥafṣ ᶜUmar ibn Isḥāq al-Hindī al-Ḥanafī (d. 773) the author of *Sharḥ al-Hidāya* and *Sharḥ al-ᶜAynī*, Najm al-Dīn al-Bahi al-Ḥanbalī (d. 802), al-Jabartī (d. 806), the major lexicographer al-Fayrūzābādī (d. 818), Shams al-Dīn al-Bisāṭī al-Māliki (d. 842), al-Munāwī (d. 871), and others. Of note regarding the above is the abundant use of Ibn ᶜArabī's sayings by al-Munāwī in his commentary of al-Suyūṭī's *Jāmiᶜ al-Ṣaghīr* entitled *Fayḍ al-Qadīr*, and by Fayrūzābādī in his commentary on Bukhārī's *al-Ṣaḥiḥ*.

Al-Suyūṭī was Ashᶜarī in his doctrine as shown in many of his works. In *Masālik al-Ḥunafā fī Wālidayy al-Muṣṭafā* ('Methods Of Those With Pure Belief Concerning the Parents of The Prophet ﷺ') he says:

The parents of the Prophet ﷺ died before he attained Prophethood, and there is no punishment for them. The Qur'an says '*We never punish until We send a messenger* [whom they reject]' (*al-Isrā'* 17: 15). Our Ashᶜarī Imams, among those in kalām, uṣūl, and fiqh, agree on the statement that one who dies while daʿwah has not reached him, dies saved. This has been explained by Imam al-Shāfiʿī as follows: ‘some of the *fuqahā’* explained that the reason for the above is, such a person follows *fitra* (primordial disposition), and has not stubbornly refused nor rejected any Messenger.’[6]

Al-Suyūṭī was taken to task for his claim that he was capable of independent scholarly exertion or *ijtihād muṭlaq*. He explained:

> I did not mean that I was similar to one of the Four Imams, but only that I was an affiliated *mujtahid* (*mujtahid muntasib*). For, when I reached the level of *tarjīh* or distinguishing the best fatwa inside the school, I did not contravene al-Nawawī’s *tarjīh*. And, when I reached the level of *ijtihad muṭlaq*, I did not contravene al-Shāfiʿī’s school.

He continued:

> There is no one in our time, on the face of the earth, from East to West, more knowledgeable than me in Hadith and the Arabic language, save al-Khidr or the Pole of saints or some other *walī* - none of whom do I include into my statement - and Allah knows best.[7]

He also said ‘When I went on hajj, I drank Zamzam water for several matters. Among them was that I reach the level of Sheikh Sirāj al-Dīn al-Bulqīnī in fiqh, and in hadith, that of hafiz Ibn Hajar.’[8]

Below are the titles of some of al-Suyūṭī’s works in print, kept in the Arabic collection of the University of Princeton in the State of New Jersey (USA). The most recent date has been given for works with more than one edition:

1. *Abwāb al Saʿāda fī Asbāb al-Shahāda* <1987> (‘The Gates of Felicity in the Causes of the Witnessing to Oneness’)

2. *Al-Ashbāh wa al-Naẓā’ir fī Furūʿ al-Shāfiʿiyya* (‘Similarities in the Branches of the Law Within the Shāfiʿī School’)

3. *Al-Ashbāh wa al-Naẓā’ir fī al-ʿArabiyya* (‘Similarities in Arabic’)

4. *Al-Aḥādīth al-Ḥisān fī Faḍl al-Ṭaylasān* <1983> (‘The Beauti-

ful Narrations Concerning the Merit of the Male Head-covering')

5. *Al-Fawz al-ʿAẓīm fī Liqā' al-Karīm* <1994> ('The Tremendous Victory in Meeting the All-Generous')
6. *Alfiyya al-Suyūṭī al-Naḥwiyya* <1900> ('The Thousand-Line Poem on Philology')
7. *Alfiyya al-Suyūṭī fī Muṣṭalah al-Ḥadīth* <1988> ('The Thousand-Line Poem on Hadith Nomenclature')
8. *ʿAmal al-Yawm wa al-Layla* <1987> ('Supererogatory Devotions for Each Day and Night')
9. *Al-Itqān fī ʿUlūm al-Qur'ān* <1996> ('Precision and Mastery in the Sciences of the Qur'an')
10. *Anīs al-Jalīs* <1874> ('The Familiar Companion')
11. *Al-'Araj fī al-Faraj* <1988> ('A Commentary on Ibn Abī al-Dunyā's "The Deliverance"', a work on hope and joy)
12. *Al-Arbaʿūn Ḥadīth fī Qawāʿid al-Aḥkām al-Sharʿiyya* <1986> ('Forty Narrations on Basic Legal Rulings')
13. *Asbāb al-Nuzūl* <1983> ('Causes of Qur'anic Revelation', verse by verse)
14. *Asbāb Wurūd al-Ḥadīth* <1988> ('Causes and Circumstances of Hadith')
15. *Isbāl al-Kisā' ʿalā al-Nisā'* <1984> ('Women and the Donning of Cover')
16. *Asrār Tartīb al-Qur'ān* <1976> ('The Secret in the Ordering of the Qur›an')
17. *Al-Āyat al-Kubra fī Sharḥ Qiṣṣat al-Isrā'* <1985> ('The Great Sign: Commentary on the Story of the Night Journey of the Prophet ﷺ')
18. *ʿAyn al-Iṣāba fī Istidrāk ʿĀ'ishah ʿalā al-Ṣaḥāba* <1988> ('Exactitude Itself in ʿĀ'isha's Rectification of the Companions')

19. *Azhār al-Mutanāthira fī al-*Aḥādīth *al-Mutawātira* <1951> ('The Most Prominent of the Reports Concerning the Narrations of Mass Transmission')

20. *Al-Bāhir fī Ḥukm al-Nabī* ﷺ <1987> ('The Dazzling Light of the Rulings of the Prophet ﷺ')

21. *Al-bahja al-marḍiyya fī sharḥ al-alfiyya* <1980> ('The pleasing beauty: a commentary on Muḥammad Ibn ʿAbdullāh Ibn Mālik›s (d. 1274 CE) "Alfiyya"', a thousand-line poem on grammar)

22. *Bulbul al-rawḍa* <1981> ('Chronicle on al-Rawda, Egypt')

23. *Bushrā al-Ka'īb bi liqā' al-Ḥabīb* <1960> ('The consolation of the sad with the meeting of the Beloved')

24. *Al-Dībāj ʿalā Ṣaḥīḥ Muslim ibn al-Ḥajjāj* <1991> ('Two-volume commentary on *Ṣaḥīḥ Muslim*')

25. *Al-Durar al-Muntathira fī al-aḥādīth al-mushtahara* <1988> ('The scattered pearls of famous narrations'); also published as *al-nawafiḥ al-ʿatira fī al-aḥādīth al-mushtahara* <1992> ('The fragrant scents of famous narrations')

26. *Al-durr al-Manthūr fī al-Tafsīr bi al-Ma'thūr* ('The scattered pearls: A commentary of Qur'an based on transmitted reports')

27. *Al-Duruj al-Munifa fī al-Abā' al-Sharīfa* <1916> ('The outstanding entries concerning the ancestors of the Prophet ﷺ')

28. *Faḍḍ al-wiʿā' fī aḥādīth rafʿ al-yadayn fī al-duʿā'* <1985> ('The emptying of the vessel concerning raising the hands when making supplication')

29. *Al-ghurar fī faḍā'il ʿUmar* <1991> ('The blazing highlights of Umar's merits')

30. *Al-Ḥabā'ik fī akhbār al-malā'ik* <1985> ('The celestial orbits or the reports concerning the angels')

31. *Ḥaqīqa al-sunna wa al-bidʿa aw al-'amr bi al-ittibāʿ wa*

al-nahī ʿan al-munkar <1985> ('The reality of Sunna and innovation or the ordering of obedient following and the prohibition of evil')

32. *Al-Ḥāwī lil-fatāwī fī al-fiqh wa-ʿulūm al-tafsīr wa al-ḥadīth wa al-uṣūl wa-al-naḥw wa al-iʿrāb wa-sā'ir al-funūn* <1933> ('The collected legal decisions in jurisprudence, Qur'anic commentary, hadith, principles, language, and other sciences')

33. *Al-ḥujaj al-mubayyana fi al-tafḍīl bayna makka wa al-madīna* <1985> ('The proofs made manifest concerning the super excellence of Makkah and Madinah')

34. *Ḥusn al-maqṣid fī ʿamal al-mawlid* <1985> ('Excellence of purpose in celebrating the birth of the Prophet ﷺ')

35. *Ḥusn al-samt fī al-ṣamt* <1985> ('The merits of silence')

36. *Iḥyā' al-mayyit bi faḍāil ahl al-bayt* <1988> ('Giving life to the dead with the merits of the Family of the Prophet ﷺ')

37. *Ikhtilāf al-madhāhib* <1989> ('The divergences among the schools of law')

38. *Al-iklīl fī istinbāṭ al-tanzīl* <1981> ('The diadem: the extraction of rulings from the revealed Book')

39. *Inbāh al-adhkiyā' fī ḥayāt al-anbiyā'* <1916> ('Notice to the wise concerning the lives of the Prophets [i.e. In the grave]')

40. *Al-iqtirāḥ fī ʿilm uṣūl al-naḥw* <1978> ('The authoritative discourse concerning the science of philology')

41. *Al-izdihār fī mā ʿaqadahu al-shuʿarā min al-aḥādīth wa al-āthār* <1991> ('The flourishes of poets related to the Prophetic narrations and sayings of the Companions')

42. *Jamʿ al-jawāmiʿ al-maʿrūf bi al-jāmiʿ al-kabīr* <1970> ('The collection of collections, known as the Major Collection')

43. *Jamiʿ al-aḥādith al-jamiʿ al-ṣaghīr wa zawā'idi* <1994> ('The Minor Collection and its addenda')

44. *Jany al-jinās* <1986> ('The genera of rhetoric')

45. *Jazīl al-mawāhib fī ikhtilāf al-madhāhib* <1992> ('The abundant gifts concerning the differences among the schools of law')

46. *Al-kanz al-madfūn wa al-falak al-mashḥūn* <1992> ('The buried treasure in the laden ship: An encyclopedia of Islamic history')

47. *Kashf al-ṣalṣala ʿan waṣf al-zalzala* <1987> ('The transmitted expositions concerning the description of the Earthquake of Doomsday')

48. *Al-Radd ʿalā man akhlada ilā al-arḍi wa jahila anna al-ijtihāda fī kulli ʿaṣrin farḍ* <1984> ('Refutation of those who cling to the earth and ignore that scholarly striving is a religious obligation in every age')

49. *Kitāb al-shamārīkh fī ʿilm al-tārīkh* <1894> ('The book of date-heavy stalks: a primer on historiography')

50. *Kitāb al-shihāb al-thāqib fi dhamm al-khalīl* <1992> ('The piercing arrows, a commentary on ʿAlī ibn Zafir's (d. 1226 CE) "The Healing of the Parched concerning the castigation of one's dear friend"', a book on the ethics of friendship)

51. *Kitāb al-tabarri min maʿarra al-maʿarrī wa tuḥfa al- ẓurafā' bi asmā' al-khulafā'* <1989> ('Poetry on the names of the Caliphs')

52. *Kitab al-tadhkīr bi al-marjiʿ wa al-maṣīr* <1991> ('Book of the reminder of the Return to Allah')

53. *Kitāb asmā' al-mudallisīn* <1992> ('The book of narrators who omit certain details while narrating')

54. *Kitāb bughya al-wuʿā fī ṭabaqāt al-lughawiyyīn* <1908> ('The must of the sagacious concerning the biographical layers of lexicologists and philologists')

55. *Kitāb hamʿ al-hawāmiʿ sharḥ jamʿ al-jawāmiʿ fī ʿilm al-naḥw* <1973> ('The rushing floodgates, or commentary on

the Collection of collections on the science of philology')

56. *Kitāb ḥusn al-muḥāḍara fī akhbār miṣr wa al-qāhira* <1904> ('The excellent lectures concerning the chronicle of Egypt and Cairo')

57. *Kitab itmām al-dirāya li qurrā' al-nuqāya* <1891> ('The perfection of knowledge for the elite among readers')

58. *Kitab lubb al-lubāb fī taḥrīr al-ansāb* <1840> ('The kernel of kernels concerning the editorship of genealogies')

59. *Tazyīn al-mamālik bi manāqib Imām Mālik* <1907> ('The adornment of slaves with the virtues of Imam Malik')

60. *Kitāb tuḥfat al-mujalis wa nuzha al-majālis* <1908> ('The jewel of every fellow student and the pleasant gatherings')

61. *Laqaṭ al-marjān fī aḥkām al-jān* <1989> ('The gleanings of coral: rulings concerning the jinn')

62. *Lubāb al-nuqūl fī asbāb al-nuzūl* <1981> ('The best of narrations concerning the circumstances of revelation')

63. *Al-lumaʿ fī khaṣā'is yawm al-jumuʿah* <1986> ('The merits of The day of jumuʿah')

64. *Mā rawāhu al-asāṭīn fī ʿadam al-majī' ilā al-salāṭīn* <1992> ('The reports concerning not appearing at the courts of rulers'); together with *Dhamm al-maks* ('The blame of taxes and tolls')

65. *Manāhil al-ṣafā fī takhrīj aḥadith al-shifā* <1988> ('The Springs of Purity: Documentation of the hadiths mentioned in Qāḍī ʿIyād's "The Healing"')

66. *Manāqib al-khulafā' al-rāshidīn* <1890> ('Virtues of the well-guided Caliphs')

67. *Al-Manhaj al-sawī wa al-manhal al-rawī fī al-ṭibb al-nabawī* <1986> ('The straight path and quenching spring: the medicine of the Prophet ﷺ)

68. *Al-maqāmat al-sundusiyya fī al-nisba al-muṣṭafawīyya*

<1916> ('The resplendent stations concerning Prophetic ancestry')

69. *Al-maṣābīḥ fī ṣalat al-tarāwīḥ* <1955> ('The lanterns of the "prayer of rests" [*tarāwīḥ*]')

70. *Masālik al-hunafā' fī waliday al-Muṣṭafā* <1993> ('Method of those of pure religion concerning the parents of the Prophet ﷺ')

71. *Al-maṭāliʿ al-saʿīda fī sharḥ al-Suyūṭī ʿalā al-alfiyya al-musamma bī al-Farida fī al-naḥw wa al-taṣrīf wa al-khaṭṭ* <1981> ('Suyūṭī's commentary on his own thousand-line poem entitled "The unique pearl" on philology, conjugation, and calligraphy')

72. *Maṭlaʿ al-badrayn fīman yu'ta ajrahu marratayn* <1991> ('The rising of the two full moons: those who are rewarded twice [i.e. Sincere Christians who accept Islam]')

73. *Miftaḥ al-jannah fī al-iʿtiṣām bi al-Sunnah* <1993> ('The key to paradise which consists in clinging to the Sunnah of the Prophet ﷺ')

74. *Mufḥimāt al-aqrān fī mubhamāt al-Qur'ān* <1991> ('The elucidations of the peers for the obscurities of the Qur'an')

75. *Al-muhadhdhab fīmā waqaʿ fī al-Qur'ān min al-muʿarrab* <1988> ('The emendation concerning the foreign words and phrases in the Qur'an')

76. *Muʿjiza maʿa karama fī kitāb al-Sharaf al-muḥattam: fī mā manna Allah taʿāla bihi ʿalā waliyyihi Aḥmad al-Rifāʿī* <1965> ('The miracle and gift concerning the book of "The paramount honour" [by al-Rifāʿī] and what Allah has bestowed in it upon His Friend Aḥmad [ibn ʿAlī] al-Rifaʿi [d. 1182 CE]')

77. *Mukhtasar sharḥ al-jamiʿ al-ṣaghīr li al-Munāwī* <1954> ('The abridged commentary of the minor collection by al-Munāwī')

78. *Muntahā al-'āmāl fī sharḥ ḥadīth innama al-aʿmāl* <1986>

('The goal of all practice, or the commentary on the hadith: Actions are according to intentions')

79. *Musnad Fātima al-zahrā' radiya allah anha wa ma warada fi faḍliha*<1994> ('The narrations traced back to Fatima the Radiant and the reports concerning her virtues')

80. *Mustaẓraf min akhbār al-jawārī* <1989> ('The graceful reports concerning women slaves')

81. *Mutawakkilī fīmā warada fī al-Qur'an bi al-lugha al-Ḥabashiyya wa al-Fārisīyya wa al-Rūmīyya wa al-Hindīyya wa al-Siryānīyya wa al-ʿIbrānīyya wa al-Nabaṭiyya wa al-Qibṭiyya wa al-Turkīyya wa al-Zanjīyya wa al-Barbarīyya* ('My reliance concerning what has been mentioned in the Qur'an in Ethiopian, Farsi, Greek, Hindi, Syriac, Hebrew, Nabatean, Coptic, Turkic, African, and Berber')

82. *Nashr al-ʿalamayn al-munīfayn fī iḥyā' al-abawayn al-sharīfayn* <1916> ('The proclamation to the two outstanding worlds [mankind and jinn] concerning the resuscitation of the parents of the Prophet ﷺ')

83. *Natīja al-fikr fī al-jahr bi al-dhikr* <1950> ('The conclusion of reflection upon loud remembrance of Allah')

84. *Naẓm al-ʿiqyān fī aʿyān al-aʿyān* <1927> ('Who's who in the ninth Hijri century')

85. *al-Nukat al-badīʿāt ʿalā al-mawḍūʿāt* <1991> (al-Suyūṭī's critique of Ibn al-Jawzi's collection of forged narrations)

86. *Nuzha al-julasā' fī ash'ār al-nisā'* <1986> ('The recreation of student gatherings concerning famous women poets')

87. *Nuzha al-muta'ammil wa-murshid al-muta'ahhil: fī al-khāṭib wa-al-mutazawwij* <1989> ('The recreation of the fiancé and the guide of the married')

88. *Nuzha al-ʿumr fī al-tafḍīl bayna al-bayḍ wa al-sumr* <1931> ('The recreation of life about establishing preference between the white and the black in complexion')

89. *Nuzul ʿĪsā ibn Maryam Ākhir al-Zamān* <1985> ('The descent of ʿĪsā ibn Maryam at the end of time')

90. *Al-qawl al-jalī fī faḍā'il ʿAlī* <1990> ('The manifest discourse on the virtues of ʿAlī ibn Abī Talib raḍiyallāhu ʿanhu')

91. *Al-raḥma fī al-ṭibb wa al-ḥikma* <1970> ('Arabic medicine and wisdom')

92. *Al-rasā'il al-ʿashr* <1989> ('The ten epistles')

93. *Raṣf al-la'āl fī wasf al-hilāl* <1890> ('The stringing of the pearls in describing the new moon')

94. *Al-rawḍ al-anīq fī fadl al-ṣiddīq* <1990> ('The beautiful garden of the merit of Abu Bakr al-Ṣiddīq raḍiyallāhu ʿanhu')

95. *Risāla al-sayf al-qāṭiʿ al-lāmiʿ li ahl al-iʿtirad al-shawa'iʿ* <1935> ('Epistle of the sharp and glistening sword to the Shīʿī people of opposition')

96. *Al-riyāḍ al-anīqa fī sharḥ asmā' khayr al-khalīqa ṣallallāhu ʿalayhi wa sallam* ('The beautiful gardens: explanation of the names of the Best of Creation [the Prophet Muhammad ﷺ]')

97. *Ṣawn al-manṭiq wa al-kalām ʿan fann al-manṭiq wa al-kalām* <1947> ('Manual of logic and dialectic theology')

98. *Shaqā'iq al-utruj fi raqā'iq al-ghunj* <1988> ('The citron halves: or, the delicacy of women')

99. *Sharḥ al-sudūr bi sharḥ ḥāl al-mawtā wa al-qubūr* <1989> ('The expanding of breasts or commentary on the state of the dead in the grave')

100. *Sharḥ al-urjūza al-musammā bi ʿuqūd al-jumān fī ʿalam al-maʿāni wa al-bayān* <1955> ('The commentary in rajāz [surging] meter entitled: The pearl necklaces related to the world of meanings and precious discourse')

101. *Sharḥ shawāhid al-mughnī* <1904> ('Commentary on the proof-texts of ʿAbdullah ibn Hishām's (d. 1360CE) *Mughnī al-labīb* or "The sufficient knowledge of the sensible one"')

102. *Shurūṭ al-mufassir wa ādābuh* <1994> ('The criteria to be met by commentators of Qur'an and their ethics')

103. *Sihām al-iṣāba fī al-daᶜawāt al-mujāba* <1987> ('The arrows that hit their target: About the prayers that are fulfilled')

104. *Subul al-jaliyya fī al-ābā' al-ᶜaliyya* <1916> ('The manifest paths concerning the lofty ancestors [of the Prophet ﷺ]')

105. *Taᶜaqqubāt al-Suyūṭī ᶜalā mawḍūᶜāt Ibn al-Jawzī* <1886> ('Suyūṭī's critique of Ibn al-Jawzī's collection of forged narrations')

106. *Ṭabaqāt al-mufassirīn* <1976> ('The biographical layers of Qur'an commentators')

107. *Tabyīḍ al-ṣaḥīfa bi manaqib al-imām Abī Ḥanīfa* <1992> ('The whitening of the page: or, the virtues of Imam Abū Ḥanīfa')

108. *Al-tadhyīl wa al-tadhnīb ᶜalā al-Nihāya fī gharīb al-ḥadīth wa al-athar* <1982> ('Marginal annotations on Ibn al-Athīr's "The goal"')

109. *Tadrīb al-rāwī fī sharḥ taqrīb al-nawawī* <1994> ('The training of the hadith transmitter: an exegesis of Nawawī's "The facilitation"')

110. *Tahdhīb al-khaṣā'iṣ al-nabawiyya al-kubra* <1989> ('The emendation of al-Suyūṭī's book entitled "The Awesome Characteristics of the Prophet ﷺ"')

111. *Taḥdhīr al-khawāṣ min akādhīb al-quṣṣāṣ* <1932> ('Warning the elite against the lies of story-tellers')

112. *Takhrīj aḥādiīth sharḥ al-mawāqif fī ᶜilm al-kalām* <1986> ('The documentation of the hadiths mentioned in "The commentary of the stopping-places in dialectical theology"', a work by Qāḍī ᶜAḍud al-Dīn ᶜAbd al-Raḥmān ibn Aḥmad Ayjī al-Shirāzī (d. 756)

113. *Tamhīd al-farsh fī al-khiṣāl al-mūjiba li-ẓilal al-ᶜarsh* <1990> ('The characteristics that guarantee the shading of the Throne')

114. *Tanbīh al-ghabī fī takhti'a ibn ʿArabī* <1990> ('Warning to the ignorant who imputes error to Muḥyi al-Dīn Ibn ʿArabī' [a reply to al-Biqāʿī's 'Warning of the ignorant that Ibn ʿArabī is a disbeliever]')

115. *Tanwīr al-ḥawālik sharḥ ʿala muwaṭṭa' Mālik* <1969> ('The enlightenment of intense blackness: a commentary on Mālik's "Trodden path"'); together with *Isʿāf al-mubaṭṭa' fī rijāl al-muwaṭṭa'* ('The succor of the stalled concerning the narrators of Mālik's "Trodden Path"')

116. *Tanwīr al-miqbas min tafsīr ibn ʿAbbās* <1951> ('The enlightenment of torchlights from the Qur'anic commentary of Ibn ʿAbbās')

117. *Tanzīh al-anbiyā' ʿan tashbīh al-aghbiyā'* <1916> ('Declaring the Prophets far above the comparisons ignorant people make of themselves with them')

118. *Taqrīr al-istinād fī tafsīr al-ijtihād* <1983> ('Establishing authoritative ascription in the course of scholarly striving')

119. *Al-taʿrīf bi ādāb al-ta'līf* <1989> ('The etiquette of authorship')

120. *Tārīkh al-khulafā'* <1993> ('History of the Caliphs')

121. *Tartīb suwar al-qur'ān* <1986> ('The disposition of the surahs of the Qur'an')

122. *Tasliya al-ābā' bi-fuqdān al-abnā' al-musamma al-taʿallul wa al-iṭfā' li-nār la tuṭfā'* <1987> ('The consolation of parents who have lost their children' also known as 'The extinction of the fire that cannot be extinguished')

123. *Ṭawq al-ḥamāma* <1988> ('The flight of the dove')

124. *Ta'yīd al-ḥaqīqa al-ʿaliyya wa tashyīd al-ṭarīqa al-shādhiliyya* <1934> ('The upholding of the lofty truth and the buttressing of the Shādhilī sufi path')

125. *Al-taʿzīm wa al-minna fī anna abaway rasūlallāh fī al-jannah* <1916> ('That the parents of the Prophet ﷺ are in Paradise')

126. *Tuḥfa al-abrār bi nukat al-adhkār li al-nawawī* <1990> ('Commentary on Nawawī's "Supplications"')

127. *Tuḥfa al-ʿAjlan fī Faḍā'il ʿUthmān* <1991> ('The merits of 'Uthmān ibn ʿAffān')

128. *Tuḥfa al-Nujabā'* <1990> ('The gem of patricians [a work on language]')

129. *ʿUqūd al-Zabarjad ʿalā Musnad al-Imam Aḥmad* <1987> ('The chrysolite necklaces on Imam Aḥmad's collection of narrations traced to the Prophet ﷺ')

130. *ʿUqūd al-Zabarjad fī Iʿr'ab al-Ḥadīth al-Nabawī* <1994> ('The chrysolite necklaces on the grammatical analysis of the narrations of the Prophet ﷺ')

131. *Al-Wasā'il fī Musāmara al-Awā'il* <1986> ('The means for conversation with the ancients'); also published as *al-Wasā'il ilā Maʿrifa al-Awā'il* <1990> ('The means to the acquaintance of the ancients')

132. *Wuṣūl al-Amānī bi Uṣūl al-Tahānī* <1987> ('The attainment of one's hope in the etiquette of well-wishing')

133. *Al-Zajr bi al-Hijr* <1950> ('The reprimand by means of the reminder of what is unlawful')

134. *Zubda al-Laban Fawa'id Lughawiyya wa Ḥadīthīyya* <1989> ('The cream of the milk: miscellaneous benefits related to language and hadith')

135. *Akhlāq Ḥamalat al-Qur'ān* <1987> ('Manners of the carriers of Qur'an')

136. *Badhl al-Himma fī Ṭalab Barā'a al-Dhimma* ('Directing one's energies to pursue clearness of conscience'); contained in the collective volume entitled: *Thalāth Rasā'il fī al-Ghība* <1988> ('Three epistles on slander')

137. *Al-la'āli' al-Maṣnūʿa fi al-Aḥādith al-Mawḍūʿa* <1960> ('The artificial pearls or forged hadiths')

138. *Daqā'iq al-akhbār fī dhikr al-jannah wa al-nār* <1961> ('The subtleties in the reports that mention Paradise and the Fire')

139. *Al-itḥāf bi ḥubb al-ashrāf* <1900> ('The present concerning love of the nobility [i.e. Descendants of the Prophet ﷺ]')

140. *Hay'a al-sanīyya fī al-hay'a al-sunnīyya* <1982> ('Treatise on astronomy')

Main sources: Ibn Fahd, *Dhayl Tadhkira al-Ḥuffāẓ* p. 6-10; al-Suyūṭī, *Tārīkh al-Khulafā'*, introduction p. 5-10; Nuh Keller, *Reliance of the Traveller* p. 1100.

NOTES

[1] Muḥammad ibn Ibrāhīm al-Shaybānī and Aḥmad al-Khazindar, eds. *Dalīl Makhṭūṭāt al-Suyūṭī*, 2nd ed. (Kuwait: *Manshūrāt Markaz al-Makhṭūṭāt*, 1995)

[2] Narrated from ʿUmar by al-Bazzār with a sound chain as stated by Haythamī

[3] See, for example, al-Sakhāwi's words in his *Maqāsid*, in the entry *khirqa*

[4] Ibn Abī Yaʿla, *Ṭabaqāt al-Ḥanābila* (1:192): 'My father (Qāḍī Abū Yaʿlā) narrated to me in writing, "Īsā ibn Muḥammad ibn ʿAlī narrated to us: I heard ʿAbdullāh ibn Muḥammad (Imam Abū al-Qāsim al-Baghawī) say: I heard Abū ʿAbdullāh Aḥmad ibn Muḥammad ibn Hanbal say: 'al-Ḥasan did narrate (*qad rawa*) from ʿAlī ibn Abī Ṭālib.'"' ʿAbd al-Razzaq in his *Muṣannaf* (7:412) narrates that Ali even consulted al-Ḥasan in a certain judicial case. For the listing of the chains of transmission establishing that al-Ḥasan narrated from Ali see al-Suyūṭī's *Ta'yīd al-Ḥaqīqa al-ʿAlīyya wa Tashyīd al-Ṭarīqa al-Shādhilīyya* and Aḥmad al-Ghumari's *al-Burhān al-Jalī fī Taḥqīq Intisāb al-Ṣūfiyya ila ʿAlī*

[5] Al-Biqāʿī, *Maṣraʿ al-Taṣawwuf aw Tanbīh Al-Ghabī Ilā Takfīr Ibn ʿArabī*, ed. ʿAbd al-Raḥmān al-Wakīl (Bilbis: Ḍār al-Taqwa, <1989>); al-Suyūṭī, *Tanbīh Al-Ghabī Fi Takhti'a Ibn ʿArabī*, ed. ʿAbd al-Raḥmān Ḥasan Maḥmūd (Cairo: Maktaba al-Adab, 1990)

[6] It is related that some of the Ashʿarī imams such as al-Qurṭubī, al-Subkī, and al-Shaʿrānī said that Abū Ṭālib, the Prophet's uncle, was also saved, according to Sheikh Aḥmad Zayni Daḥlān in his epistle *Asnā al-Maṭālib fī Najāt Abī Ṭālib* (Cairo: Muḥammad Effendi Muṣṭafā, 1305/1886) who cites Imam al-Suḥaymī and the Ḥanafī Mufti of Makkah Sheikh Aḥmad ibn ʿAbdullāh Mīrghanī to that effect. They mention, among other evidence, the narration of al-ʿAbbās (*raḍiyallāhu ʿanhu*). Ibn Saʿd said in his *Ṭabaqāt al-Kūbra* (1:118):

ʿAffān ibn Muslim told us: Ḥammād ibn Salama told us: from Thābit [ibn Aslam al-Bunānī]: from Iṣḥāq ibn ʿAbdullāh ibn al-Ḥārith [ibn Nawfal] who said: al-ʿAbbās said: 'I said: "O Messenger of Allah, do you hope anything for Abū Ṭālib?" He replied: "I hope everything good from my Lord."' The above narrators are all trustworthy and their transmission is sound, except that the meaning of the hadith is vague. Further, al-Qurṭubī, in his *tafsīr* (for verses 6:26 and 9:53) and Ibn al-Subkī in *Ṭabaqāt al-Shāfiʿīyya al-Kūbra* (1:91-94) hold different positions than those ascribed to them above, and the sound evidence to the contrary is explicit and abundant, but Allah knows best

[7] Al-Suyūṭī, *al-Radd ʿalā man Akhlada ila al-Arḍ* (p. 116)

[8] Al-Suyūṭī, *Ḥusn al-Muḥāḍara fī Akhbar Miṣr wa al-Qāhira* (p. 157)

Shedding Light on the Possibility of Seeing Prophets and Angels

Tanwīr al-Ḥalak fī Imkān Ru'yah al-Nabī wa al-Malak

by Imam Jalāl al-Dīn al-Suyūṭī

Translated by

Talut ibn Sulaiman Dawood

In the Name of Allah, the Beneficent, the Merciful

All praise is due to Allah. Peace be upon His chosen servants

To proceed:

We have received numerous inquiries regarding people in spiritual states observing the waking vision of the Prophet ﷺ. Indeed, a party of the people of this age, among those who have no foothold in knowledge, vehemently denied the possibility of that. They are astonished by it and claim that it is impossible. So, I have written this short work and named it 'Dispelling the Darkness Regarding the Possibility of Seeing Prophets and Angels' [Tanwīr al-Ḥalak fī Imkān Ru'yah al-Nabī wa al-Malak]."

We begin with the *ṣaḥīḥ* hadith narrated regarding it. Al-Bukhārī, Muslim and Abū Dāwūd narrated that Abū Hurayrah (*raḍiyallāhu ʿanhu*) said, 'The Messenger of Allah ﷺ said, "If someone sees me in a dream, he will soon see me while awake. Satan cannot imitate my form."' Al-Ṭabarānī narrated something similar from the hadith of Mālik ibn ʿAbdullāh al-Khathaʿmī and the hadith of Abū Bakrah. And, al-Dārimī narrated the same from the hadith of Abū Qatāda.

The scholars say that people disagreed over the meaning of his words, 'He will soon see me while awake.' Some said that its meaning is, 'He will see me on the Day of Judgement.' However, they are rebuked by the argument that there would be no benefit to such an allotment, because all of his *ummah* will see him on the Day of Judgement, regardless of whether or not they had seen him in a dream.

It has also been said that the meaning is that if someone believes in him during his life, despite the fact that he has not seen him due to his being hidden from him, it is a glad tiding that he would inevitably see him while awake, before his death. However, another group said that it is understood according to its apparent meaning. Thus, whoever sees him in a dream, he will without doubt see him while awake, meaning his physical eyes. It is also said that such a vision is with the eyes of the heart. Both positions were reported from Qāḍī Abū Bakr ibn al-ʿArabī.

Imam Abū Muḥammad ibn Abī Jamrah said, in his comments on the hadiths that he selected from al-Bukhārī:

> This hadith indicates that if anyone sees him ﷺ in a dream, he will see him while awake. However, does it indicate both during his life and after he has passed away? Or, is it restricted to those who lived during his lifetime? Also, is this [benefit] for anyone who sees him without exception, or is it restricted to those who are deserving by following His Sunnah ﷺ?
>
> The wording indicates that it is a general and unrestricted statement. And, those who claim that it is restricted, without any indication of that restriction from him ﷺ, are transgressing their limits. Some people had fallen into [the trap of] not confirming its general meaning, saying, according to the conclusion of their intellect, 'How could someone who has passed away be seen in the physical world by those who are living?'
>
> Such a statement is perilous from two important points of view. The first is that it contains a refusal to confirm the words of the Truthful One ﷺ, who does not speak from a place of desires. The second is that it indicates ignorance of the power of the Almighty and a belief that His power is deficient. It is as if he has not heard the story of the cow in surah al-Baqarah, how Allah (*ta ʿālā*) said *'We said: Strike him with a part of it. In such a way, Allah will give life to the dead person'* (*al-Baqarah* 2: 73). Or, the story of Ibrāhīm (*ʿalayhi al-salām*) and the four birds, or the story of ʿUzayr. For, the One who made the striking of the dead person with a piece of the cow a means to bringing him back to life; the summoning of Ibrāhīm a means to giving life to the birds; and the astonishment of Uzair a means to his death, the death of his donkey and to reviving them both after one hundred years, is certainly able to make seeing him ﷺ in a dream a means to seeing him while awake.
>
> It has been narrated about one of the Companions, who I believe to be Ibn ʿAbbās (*raḍiyallāhu ʿanhumā*), that he saw the Prophet ﷺ in a dream. It caused him to remember that hadith and he kept thinking about it. Then, he entered upon one of the wives of the Prophet ﷺ, who I believe was Maymūnah,

and he told her what had happened. So, she got up and took out the mirror of the Prophet ﷺ. He (*raḍiyallāhu ʿanhu*) said, 'I looked into the mirror and saw his image and I did not see my own image.'

And there are many people among the Predecessors and the following generations, and all those up to this time, who have been mentioned as having seen him ﷺ. They were among those who were truthful about such events and they saw him after that while awake. They asked him about matters about which they were confused and he informed them of the solution and of the different ways to arrive at it (the solution). And, they corroborated the solution in the manner described without any addition.

The negater of this [vision] is either someone who confirms the *karāmāt* of the Saints or denies them. If he is among those who denies them, there is no need to discuss the matter with him, because he has denied a matter that the Sunnah has confirmed with clear evidences. However, if he is among those who confirms their *karāmāt*, this vision is from that category because the Saints are unveiled, by way of preternatural events, to various matters concerning the upper and lower realms and this vision cannot be denied while confirming such unveiling.

His words explain that it is a general statement, not restricted to those who are deserving of it or who follow his Sunnah ﷺ more closely. This means that the vision while awake, which was promised for those who saw him in a dream, will occur - even if only once - as a confirmation of his noble promise which is never broken. For the general believers, the least that will occur is that when his death draws near, he will see him before his spirit departs from his body. He will see him as a fulfilment of this promise. As for others, they will receive the vision throughout their lifetime, either many times, or a few times, according to their efforts and observation of the Sunnah. However, neglecting the Sunnah is a great impediment to this benefit.

Muslim narrated in his *al-Ṣaḥīḥ* that Muṭarraf said, "ʿImrān ibn Ḥuṣayn said to me, "I was being greeted with peace until I used cauterization. When I abandoned cauterization, my greetings returned."' Muslim narrated from another chain of narration that Muṭarraf said, "ʿImrān ibn Ḥuṣayn sent for me during his final illness. He said to me,

"I will tell you something. If I live, then conceal it. But if I die, relate it if you wish. I used to receive greetings of peace.'"

Al-Nawawī said, in his explanation of Muslim:

> The meaning of the first hadith is that ʿImrān ibn Ḥuṣayn suffered from haemorrhoids and he bore their pain patiently. Thus, the Angels would greet him with peace. Then, he cauterized them, and they ceased their greetings. Then, he abandoned cauterization and the Angels returned to greeting him with peace. His words in the second hadith, 'If I live, then conceal it for me,' refer to not informing others that he was being greeted with peace, because he hated that that should be widely known about him in his lifetime, since that would expose him to *fitnah*, as opposed to after his death.

Al-Qurṭubī said, in is explanation of Muslim, '[The hadith] means that the Angels had been greeting him with peace, out of honour and veneration for him, until he applied cauterization. They then stopped greeting him. And in this hadith, there is a confirmation of the *karāmāt* of the Saints.'

Al-Ḥākim related, declaring it sound in his *Mustadrak*, by way of al-Muṭarraf ibn ʿAbdullāh that ʿImrān ibn Ḥuṣayn said, 'You should know, O, Muṭarraf, that the Angels used to greet me with peace near my head, near my house and at the door to my room. However, when I applied cauterization, that [benefit] departed.' And when he had freed himself of that, I spoke to him and he said, 'You should know, O, Muṭarraf, that what I mentioned to you has returned. But conceal it until my death.'

Consider how ʿImran was veiled from hearing the greetings of the Angels due to his having used cauterization, despite the immense necessity of doing so, because cauterization goes against the Sunnah. Al-Bayhaqī stated in *Shuʿab al-Īmān*:

> If the interdiction of cauterization had been by way of prohibition, ʿImran would never have used it despite the fact that it had been interdicted. However, since he performed a disliked act, the Angles who had been greeting him with peace parted company from him. At that he became depressed, so he said what he said. But it has been narrated that he returned to doing that before his death.

Ibn Athīr said, in *al-Nihāyah*:

> It means that the Angels would greet him with peace. But, when he applied cauterization because of his illness, they abandoned greeting him. That is because cauterization is a deficiency in one's reliance and submission to Allah, in patient perseverance with that with which He afflicts the slave, and in seeking one's cure from Him alone. That doesn't mean that cauterization is illicit. Rather, it is only a deficiency in one's reliance, which is a lofty degree beyond the use of intermediary means.

Ibn Saᶜd narrated in his *Ṭabaqāt* on the authority of Qatādah, that the Angels used to shake ᶜImran ibn Ḥuṣayn's hands until he applied cauterization. [When he did that], they avoided him.

Abū Naᶜīm narrated in *Dalā'il al-Nubuwwah* that Yaḥya ibn Saᶜīd al-Qaṭṭān said, 'No Companion came to us in Baṣrah, better than ᶜImrān ibn Ḥuṣayn. The Angels came to him for over thirty years greeting him with peace near to his house.' Al-Tirmidhī narrated in his history, and Abū Naᶜīm and al-Bayhaqī both narrated in [their respective books] *Dalā'il al-Nubuwwah* that Ghazālah said, "ᶜImrān ibn Ḥuṣayn used to order us to sweep his home. And we would hear, 'Peace be upon you. Peace be upon you.' But we wouldn't see anyone.' Al-Tirmidhī said, 'That was the greeting of the Angels.'

Hujjat al-Islām Abū Ḥāmid al-Ghazālī said, in his book *al-Munqidh min al-Ḍalāl*:

> When I became unoccupied by studies, I turned my aspiration towards the path of the Sufis. And what I wish to mention, so that people may benefit from it, is that I understood with certainty that the Sufis are the wayfarers on the paths of Allah, that their journey and method are the most excellent of journeys, that their path is the most excellent path, and that their conduct is the purest. In fact, if the intellect of the intellectuals, the wisdom of the wise, and the knowledge of those scholars who discover the secrets of the Sacred Law were gathered in order to change something of their method and conduct, or to replace it for something better than it, they would not find any way to do that. All their states of activity and inactivity are plucked from the niche of the light of Prophecy. And there is, beyond the light of Prophecy, no light on the face of the earth by which one may seek illumination.

The description continues up to his words, 'Until they, while awake, witness the Angels and the spirits of the Prophets. They hear their voices and they take lessons from them. And then their state of witnessing is elevated from witnessing forms and appearances, to levels which are very difficult to articulate.'

His student, Abū Bakr ibn al-ʿArabī, one of the Imams of the Mālikīs said in his book *Qānūn al-Ta'wīl*:

> The Sufis opined, that when a person attains purity of the soul and purification of the heart, cuts off all attachments and severs the evil ties of the world, such as status, wealth and unnecessary associations, and turns to Allah (*ta ʿālā*) completely, perpetually in his knowledge and constantly in his actions, hearts will be unveiled to him, he will see the Angels and hear their speech, and he will see the spirits of the Prophets and listen to their words.

Then he said, 'Seeing the Prophets and Angels and hearing their speech is possible for the believer as an ennoblement and for the disbeliever as a punishment.'

Sheikh ʿIzz al-Dīn ibn ʿAbd al-Salām said in *al-Qawā'id al-Kubrā*:

> Ibn al-Hājj said, in *al-Madkhal*, 'Seeing the Prophet ﷺ while awake is a narrow door. Few people will experience it, except the one who has a very rare attribute in this time. Rather, that attribute is non-existent for the most part. However, we do not deny that it can occur to some elevated Saints whose inner and outer being Allah has protected. Some of the scholars of the exterior rulings had negated the vision of the Prophet ﷺ while awake. They reasoned that the temporal essence cannot see the permanent essence. The Prophet ﷺ is in the abode of permanence while the one who [ostensibly] sees him is in the ephemeral abode. However, Sīdī Abū Muhammīd ibn Abī Jamrah had removed this problem and refuted it by the fact that the believer will see Allah after he dies, while Allah does not die. And every one of them dies seventy times a day."

Qāḍī Sharaf al-Dīn Hibah Allah ibn ʿAbd al-Raḥīm al-Bārizī said, in his book *Tawthīq ʿUra al-Īmān*:

> Al-Bayhaqī said, in his *Kitāb al-Iʿtiqād*, 'After the Prophets are caused to pass away, their spirits are returned to them. So, they are alive with their Lord, like the martyrs. And our Prophet ﷺ saw a number of them on the night of Miʿrāj. And, he stated, and his statements are all true, that our prayers upon him are presented before him, and our greetings are delivered to him. And he stated that Allah (*ta ʿālā*) has prevented the earth from consuming the flesh of the Prophets.'

Al-Bārizī stated, 'We have heard of a group of the Saints of our time and prior to this time, that saw the Prophet ﷺ alive, while awake, after his death.' This was mentioned by Sheikh al-Islām, Imam Abū al-Bayān ibn Muḥammad ibn Mahfūẓ al-Dimashqī in his *Nazīmah*.

Sheikh Akmal al-Dīn al-Bābartī al-Ḥanafī said in his *Sharḥ al-Mashāriq* on the hadith, '*If someone sees me in a dream…*'[1]

> The meeting of two people in wakefulness or in a dream is due to factor that unifies them. And those factors have five universal bases: sharing in a single being, in one or more attributes, in one or more states, in actions or in degree. All the conceivable relationships between two things, or between many things, return without exception to these five. And in accordance with the domination of that which makes them similar over that which makes them different, or its being dominated by them, their meetings will be plentiful or few. And one characteristic may dominate its opposite, such that love may increase to the point that two people become nearly inseparable. Or, it could be the opposite. But if someone attains all five fundamental factors with regard to the spirits of the perfect people of the past, and their relationship becomes confirmed, he may meet with them whenever he wants.

Sheikh Ṣafī al-Dīn ibn Abī al-Manṣūr said in his *Risālah*, and Sheikh ʿAfīf al-Dīn al-Yāfiʿī said in *Rawḍ al-Rayāḥīn*:

> The Great Sheikh, the Exemplar of the Gnostic Shaykhs and the blessing of the people of his time, Abū ʿAbdullāh al-Qurashī said, 'When great misguidance afflicted the abodes of Egypt,

1 That is the hadith mentioned above, from al-Bukhārī, '*If someone sees me in a dream, he will soon see me while awake…*'

> I concentrated on supplicating. It was said to me, "Don't supplicate. For none of your supplications regarding this matter will be granted." So, I travelled to Sham and when I came close to the grave of the *Khalīl* ﷺ, the *Khalīl* met me and I said to him, "O, Messenger of Allah! As I am your guest, supplicate for the people of Egypt." So, he supplicated for them and Allah granted them relief.'

Al-Yāfiʿī then said, 'His words "The Khalīl met me…" are true and are only negated by an ignorant person who has no knowledge of the states that overcome them, in which they witness the inner dominion of the Heavens and the Earth and see the Prophets as living and not dead, just as the Prophet ﷺ saw Mūsā (*ʿalayhi al-salām*) on Earth, and then saw him and a group of Prophets in the Heavens. And he heard their speech. And it has been confirmed that whatever is possible for the Prophets as a prophetic miracle is also possible for the Saints as a saintly miracle. However, the latter does not occur in response to a challenge.

Sheikh Sirj al-Dīn ibn al-Mulaqqin said in his *Ṭabaqāt al-Awliyā'*:

> Sheikh ʿAbd al-Qādir al-Kaylānī said, 'I saw the Messenger of Allah ﷺ before Ẓuhr, and he said to me, "O, my son! Why do you not speak?" I said, "O, my father! I am a non-Arab. How can I speak before the eloquent Arabic speakers of Baghdad?" He said, "Open your mouth." So, I opened it and he spit in it seven times. Then, he said, "Speak to people. And call to the path of your Lord with wisdom and beautiful sermons." So, I prayed Ẓuhr and sat and a large group of people came to me. But I became confused. Then, I saw ʿAli standing opposite me in the gathering. He said to me, "O, my son! Why do you not speak?" I said, "O, my father! I have become perplexed." So, he said to me, "Open your mouth." I opened it and he spit into it six times. I said to him, "Why did you not complete the seven times?" He said, "Out of courtesy to the Messenger of Allah ﷺ." Then, he disappeared from me and I said, "Penetrating thought dives into the ocean of the heart for pearls of gnosis. And extracts them to the shore of the chest, where the translator of the tongue calls to them and sells them for the price of breaths spent in excellent obedience, in the houses that Allah has allowed to be raised."'

He (Ibn al-Mulaqqin) also said, in the biography of Sheikh Khalīfah ibn Mūsā al-Nahr Milkī:

> He would frequently see the Messenger of Allah ﷺ in both wakefulness and dreams. And, it is said that he received the majority of his practice through a Prophetic order, either while awake or in dreams. In one night, he saw him seventeen times. He said to him, on one of those times, "O, Khalīfah! Do not become vexed with me. There are Saints who have died of anxiousness to see me."

Al-Kamāl al-Udfuwī mentioned in *al-Ṭali' al-Saʿīd*, in the biography of al-Safi Abū ʿAbdullāh ibn Yaḥyā al-Aswānī:

> He lived in Akhmīm. And he is from the companions of Abū Yaḥyā ibn Shāfiʿ. He was famous for his piety and had many unveilings and Karāmāt. Ibn Daqīq al-ʿĪd, Ibn Niʿmān and the Quṭb al-ʿAsqalānī said about him, 'He would mention that he used to see the Prophet ﷺ and meet with him.'

Sheikh ʿAbd al-Ghaffār ibn Nūḥ al-Qūṣi said in his book, *al-Waḥīd*, 'He was from the companions of Sheikh Abū Yaḥyā Abū ʿAbdullāh al-Aswānī who lived in Akhmīm. He would relate that he used to see the Messenger of Allah ﷺ every hour, to such an extent that nearly no hour would pass without him speaking about him.'

The author of *al-Waḥid* also said, 'Abū al-ʿAbbās al-Mursī had a communion with the Prophet ﷺ, such that when he greeted the Prophet ﷺ, he would respond to his greeting, and when he spoke to him, he would answer him."

Sheikh Tāj al-Dīn ibn ʿAta' Allah said, in *Laṭā'if al-Minan*:

> A man said to Sheikh Abū al-ʿAbbās al-Mursī, 'O, my Master! Shake my hand with your palm. For you have met such and such a person and seen such and such a land.' He replied, 'By Allah! I have not shaken the hand of anyone, with this palm, other than the Messenger of Allah ﷺ.'

The Sheikh also said, 'If the Messenger of Allah ﷺ were veiled from me for the blinking of an eye, I would not count myself among the Muslims.'

Sheikh Ṣafī al-Dīn ibn Abī al-Manṣūr said, in his *Risālah,* and Sheikh ʿAbd al-Ghaffār said in his *al-Waḥīd*:

> Sheikh Abū al-Ḥasan al-Wannani said, 'Sheikh Abū al-ʿAbbās al-Tanjī informed me: "Sīdī Aḥmad al-Rifāʿī said to me, 'I am not your sheikh. Your sheikh is ʿAbd al-Rahīm in Qinā.' So, I traveled to Qinā and entered upon Sheikh ʿAbd al-Rahīm. He asked me, "Do you know the Messenger of Allah ﷺ?" I said, "No." He said, "Travel to Bayt al-maqdis." And when I planted my two feet, behold, the Heaven, the Earth, the Throne and the Footstool were all filled with the Messenger of Allah ﷺ!" So, I returned to the Sheikh and he asked me, "Do you know the Messenger of Allah ﷺ?" I said, "Yes." He said, "Then, your path is complete. The Quṭbs were not Quṭbs, the Awtād were not Awtād and none of the Saints were Saints, except through the knowledge of the Messenger of Allah ﷺ."'

The author of *al-Waḥīd* said:

> Among those who I saw in Makkah was Sheikh ʿAbdullāh al-Dallāṣī. He informed me that, in his entire life, only one of his prayers had been valid. He said, 'That was when I was in Masjid al-Haram, praying the dawn prayer. When the Imam performed the *takbīr taḥrīmah* and I followed him in that, I was seized by a state and saw the Messenger of Allah ﷺ praying in front of me, with the ten who were promised paradise behind him. So, I prayed with them. That was in the year 673 AH. In the first *rakʿah*, he ﷺ recited surah al-Muddaththir and in the second al-Nabaʾ. And, when he ended the prayer, he prayed with the following supplication: "O, Allah! make us guided guides. Do not make us misguided or misguiding, covetous by your generosity nor desirous of that which is with you, because Your grace was upon us before You created us and before we came to be. Thus, to You belongs all praise for that. There is no god but You." When the Prophet ﷺ finished, the Imam ended the prayer, and I recognized his *taslīm*, so I too ended the prayer.'

Sheikh Ṣafī al-Dīn said, in his *Risālah*:

> Sheikh Abū al-ʿAbbās al-Ḥadād said, 'I entered upon the Prophet ﷺ once. I found him writing down those Saints whose sainthood was known publicly. He wrote down my brother Muḥammad among the famous Saints.' His brother was a great Saint. He had a light on his face that made his sainthood evident to everyone. So, we asked the Sheikh about that. He said, 'The Messenger of Allah ﷺ blew into my face. And that breath left the mark of this light.'

Sheikh Ṣafī al-Dīn also said:

> I saw the great, majestic Sheikh, Abū ʿAbdullāh al-Qurṭubī, one of the greatest of the companions of Sheikh al-Qurashī. He lived most of the time in Madinah. And he used to commune with the Prophet ﷺ, receive answers from him and hear his returned greeting. The Messenger of Allah ﷺ once charged him to take a letter to the king, al-Kāmil. He went to Egypt with that letter, delivered it and returned to Madinah. He said, 'Among those who I saw in Egypt was the Sheikh Abū al-ʿAbbās al-ʿAsqalānī, one of the most elect of the companions of Sheikh al-Qurashī, the ascetic of Egypt of his time.' Most of his time at the end of his life was spent in Makkah. It is said that once he entered upon the Messenger of Allah ﷺ, and the Prophet ﷺ said to him, 'May Allah take you by the hand, O, Aḥmad.'

It has also been narrated about one Saint that he was present in the gathering of one jurist. The jurist narrated a hadith but the Saint said to him, 'That hadith is false.' The jurist asked him, 'How did you determine that?' He said, 'The Prophet ﷺ is standing over you and saying, "I never said that hadith."' The veils were thus lifted from the jurist and he saw him.

In the book *al-Minaḥ al-Ilahiyyah fi Manāqib Sādat al-Wafā'iyyah* of Ibn Fāris, the author said:

> I heard Sīdī ʿAli (*raḍiyallāhu ʿanhu*) saying, 'At the age of five, I used to recite the Qur'an to a man who was called Sheikh Yaʿqūb. One day, I came to him and I saw the Prophet ﷺ, while awake and not asleep. He was wearing a white, cotton shirt. Then, I saw the same shirt upon myself. He then said to me, "Recite." So, I recited surah al-Ḍuḥā and surah al-Sharh. He

then disappeared. When I reached twenty-one years of age, I performed the *taḥrīmah* for the morning prayer in Qarāfah. And I saw the Prophet ﷺ in front of me. He embraced me and said, "*As for the blessing of your Lord, declare it*" *(ad-Duḥā 93: 11)*. From that time, I was given his speech.'

Sīdī al-Hajj Aḥmad al-Rifāʿī said, in one of his Majāmiʿ:

When my spirit was remote [from this place], I would send it forth,
To kiss its earth on my behalf, for it is my representative,
But now, the physical form that was represented is present,
So, stretch out your right hand that I may touch it with my two lips.
Thus, the noble hand came out of the grave and he kissed it.

Sheikh Burhān al-Dīn al-Biqāʿī said, in his Muʿjam:

Imam Abū al-Faḍl ibn Abī al-Faḍl al-Nawīrī narrated to us that when Sayyed Nūr al-Dīn al-Ayjī, the father of the Sharīf ʿAfīf al-Dīn arrived at the noble grave and said, 'Peace be upon you, O, Prophet, and the mercy of Allah and His blessings', those who were present with him heard a voice coming from the grave, saying, 'And upon you be peace, O, my son.'

Hafiz Muḥibb al-Dīn ibn Najjār said in his history book:

Abū Aḥmad Dawūd ibn ʿAlī ibn Hibat Allah ibn Maslamah informed us that Abū al-Faraj al-Mubārak ibn ʿAbdullāh ibn Muḥammad ibn al-Nuqur said, 'Our Sheikh, Abū Naṣr ʿAbd al-Wahīd ibn ʿAbd al-Mālik ibn Muḥammad ibn Abī Saʿd al-Sufī al-Karkhī told us, "I performed Hajj and visited the Prophet ﷺ. While we were sitting next to the [Prophetic] apartment, Sheikh Abū Bakr al-Dayyār Bakrī entered, stood adjacent to the face of the Prophet ﷺ and said, 'Peace be upon you, O, Messenger of Allah.' and I heard a voice from inside of the apartment say, 'And upon you be peace, O, Abū Bakr.' And all those who were present heard it."'

In the book *Misbāḥ al- Ẓulām fī al-Mustaghīthīna bi Khayr al-Anām*, by Shams al-Dīn Muḥammad ibn Mūsā ibn Nuʿman, the author said:

> I heard Yūsuf ibn ʿAli al-Zinātī tell the story of a Hashimite woman who was a resident of Madinah. Some of the servants would abuse her. So, she said, 'I sought help from the Prophet ﷺ. And I heard a voice from the grave saying, "Are you not from my family? So, be patient as I was patient," or something with the same meaning. Thus, my affliction was removed from me and the three servants who had been abusing me died.'

In the *Dalā'il*, Ibn al-Samʿānī said:

> Abū al-Qāsim ʿAbd al-Raḥmān ibn ʿUmar ibn Tamīm al-Mu'adhdhan informed us that ʿAlī ibn Ibrāhim ibn ʿAllān narrated to him that ʿAlī ibn Muḥammad ibn ʿAli informed him that Aḥmad ibn al-Haytham al-Ṭā'ī narrated to him that his father narrated to him on the authority of his father, on the authority of Salama ibn Kuhal, on the authority of Abū Ṣādiq, that ʿAlī ibn Abī Ṭālib (*raḍiyallāhu ʿanhu*) said, 'A Bedouin came to us after we had buried the Messenger of Allah ﷺ. He threw himself upon the grave of the Prophet ﷺ and sprinkled some of its dust on his head. Then he said, "O, Messenger of Allah! You have spoken and we have listened. You received from Allah [what you received]. And we received from you [what we received]. Among that which was revealed upon you by Allah is '*If, after they had wronged themselves, they would have come to you, and sought the forgiveness of Allah and the Messenger would have sought forgiveness for them, they would have found Allah oft-accepting of repentance, Very Merciful*' [*al-Nisā*' 4: 64]. I have certainly wronged myself. And I have come to you that you may seek forgiveness for me." A call came from the grave that he had been forgiven.'

I have also seen the following text, in the book *Muzīl al-Shubuhāt fī Ithbāt al-Karāmāt* of Imam ʿImād al-Dīn Ismāʿīl ibn Hibat Allah ibn Bāṭīsh:

> Among the evidences that confirm the Karāmāt, are some traditions that have been transmitted from the Companions and the Tābiʿīn, and those after them. Among them is Imam Abu Bakr al-Ṣiddīq (*raḍiyallāhu ʿanhu*). He said to ʿĀ'ishah (*raḍiyallāhu ʿanhā*), 'They are your two brothers and your

two sisters.' She replied, 'My two brothers are Muḥammad and ʿAbd al-Raḥmān. But who are my two sisters, when my only sister is Asmā'?' he replied, 'I have been inspired that the child which the daughter of Khārijah is carrying is a girl.' And Umm Kulthūm was born.

Also, among them, is ʿUmar ibn al-Khaṭṭāb (*raḍiyallāhu ʿanhu*) in the story of Sāriyah, when he said, while giving the *khutbah*, 'O, Sāriyah! The mountain! The mountain!' And Allah caused Sāriyah to hear his words while he was in Nahavand. There is also a story related about him and the Nile river. He sent a messenger to it and it began to flow after it had stopped.

There is also the story of ʿUthmān ibn ʿAffān (*raḍiyallāhu ʿanhu*). ʿAbdullāh ibn Salām said, 'I then came to ʿUthmān ibn 'Affān (*raḍiyallāhu ʿanhu*), while he was besieged, to greet him with peace. He said, "Welcome, my brother. I saw the Messenger of Allah ﷺ in that window. He said, 'O, Uthman! They have besieged you.' I said, 'Yes.' He said, 'They have caused you thirst.' I said, 'Yes.' So, he brought me a container with water. I drank to my fill, until I felt its coolness between my two breasts and between my two shoulder blades. Then, he said to me, 'If you prefer, you will be given victory against them. Or, if you wish, you may break your fast with us.' I elected to break my fast with him." And he was killed on that day.'

This story is well-known and famous, narrated in the books of Hadith with the *isnād* by which it was narrated in the *Musnad* of al-Ḥārith ibn Abī Usāmah. And the author [of *Muzīl al-Shubuhāt fī Ithbāt al-Karāmāt*] has understood this vision to be while awake. If not, then it would not be proper to mention it among *karāmāt*, because there is no distinction among people regarding the ability to see [him] in a dream. It is not among the preternatural events that are numbered among the *karāmāt*. And, even those who deny *karāmāt* do not deny it (the possibility of seeing him in a dream).

Something else that Ibn Bāṭīsh said in the abovementioned book is the following:

Among them is Abū al-Ḥusayn Muḥammad ibn Samʿūn al-Baghdadi al-Ṣūfī. Abū Ṭāhir Muḥammad ibn ʿAlī al-ʿAllān said, 'I visited Abū al-Ḥusayn ibn Samʿūn one day in his gath-

> ering of counsels. He was sitting upon his chair speaking. And Abū al-Fatḥ al-Qawās was sitting on one side of his chair. He was overtaken by drowsiness and slept. So, Abū al-Ḥusayn stopped speaking for an hour until Abū al-Fatḥ woke up and raised his head. Abū al-Ḥusayn said to him, 'You saw the Prophet ﷺ in your dream.' He said, 'Yes'. He said to him, 'That is why I stopped speaking for an hour, out of fear that I would disturb you and cut off your experience.'

This intimates that Ibn Samᶜūn saw the Prophet ﷺ when he was present and Abū al-Fatḥ saw him in his dream.

And Abū Bakr ibn Abyaḍ said in his short work:

> I heard Abū al-Hasan Bannāna al-Kamāl al-Zāhid saying, 'One of our companions narrated to me that there was a man in Makkah who was called Ibn Thābit. He had left Makkah for Madinah for sixty years, with only the intention of greeting the Prophet ﷺ and then returning. However, during that time, he was delayed by some business, or for some reason. He said that when he finally sat before the [Prophetic] apartment, while he was between sleep and wakefulness, he saw the Prophet ﷺ. He was saying to him, "O, Ibn Thābit! You did not visit us. For we visited you."'

SOME IMPORTANT POINTS

The **first** is that the vision of the Prophet ﷺ while awake occurs most often with the heart. Then, one is raised to the point that he sees him with his eyes. And we have already mentioned what Qāḍī Abū Bakr ibn al-ᶜArabī had to say about both kinds of visions. However, the vision with the eyes is not like the ordinary vision known among people, where one of them may see the other. It is a meeting that takes place due to a spiritual state, a spiritual experience of the Barzakh, and an ecstatic state that is only known by those who experience it. And we mentioned what was related by Sheikh ᶜAbdullāh al-Dallāṣī, '... when the Imam performed the *taḥrīmah*, I also performed it. Then, I was overtaken by a state and saw the Messenger of Allah ﷺ ...' With the words, '... I was overtaken by a state,' he was alluding to the aforementioned state.

The **second**, is whether or not the vision is of the being of the Messenger of Allah ﷺ in both spirit and body. Or, if it is a semblance of him. The people of spiritual states that have seen him say that it is the latter. Al-Ghazālī explicitly stated that, saying:

> The meaning is not that someone sees his physical body. Rather, it is a semblance. And that semblance became a means by which one perceives the meaning that is within himself. At times, that tool may be real. And at times it is an imaginary form. But the self is not an imaginary semblance. Thus, the form one sees is not the spirit of the Chosen One, nor his person. Rather, it is confirmed to be a semblance of him.

He continued:

> Similar to this is when someone sees Allah (*ta ͨālā*) in a dream. His Essence is exalted above shape and form. However, he is acquainted with him by means of a perceptible semblance, such as light or something else. But that semblance will be true in its being a means to knowing. Thus, the one who sees such a dream will say, 'I have seen Allah in a dream.' Yet, he will not mean that he has seen the Essence of Allah, as he would say with created beings.

However, Qāḍī Abū Bakr ibn al-ͨArabī made a distinction, saying, 'If someone sees the Prophet ﷺ in his well-known description, it will be a real perception, while if he sees him upon a different description, then it will be a perception of that semblance.' And, this saying of his is very excellent because there is no impediment to seeing his noble being in body and spirit because he ﷺ, and all the rest of the Prophets, are alive. Their spirits are returned to them after they have passed away. And, they are given permission to leave their graves and influence the upper and lower realms of the Divine Kingdom.

Al-Bayhaqī authored a short work on the life of the Prophets. He also said, in *Dalā'il al-Nubuwwah*, 'The Prophets are alive with their Lord like the martyrs.' And he said, in *Kitāb al-Iͨtiqād*:

> After the Prophets pass away, their spirits are returned to them. So, they are alive with their Lord like the martyrs. Ustadh Abū Manṣūr ͨAbd al-Qāhir ibn Ṭāhir al-Baghdādī said, 'The theo-

> logical researchers among our companions have determined that our Prophet ﷺ is alive after his passing away, that he is elated by the acts of obedience of his nation and saddened by the disobedient among them, and that the prayer of whoever prays upon him from his nation is conveyed to him.'
>
> He also said that the Prophets do not disintegrate, nor does the earth consume any part of them. Mūsā passed away in his time and our Prophet ﷺ informed us that he saw him praying in his grave on the night of Ascension, and that he saw him again in the fourth heaven. He also saw Ādam and Ibrāhīm. If this foundation is valid for us, then we say that our Prophet ﷺ has become alive after his passing away. And he retains his Prophethood.

Al-Qurṭubī said, transmitting from his sheikh, in *al-Tadhkirah*, on the hadith of the swooning:

> Death is not complete nonbeing. It is only the transference from one state to another. This is demonstrated by the fact that, after the martyrs are killed and die, they are alive, provided for, elated, and rejoicing. And that is the attribute of the living in this world. If that is the case of the martyrs, the Prophets are more deserving of that. It is authentic that the earth does not consume the bodies of the Prophets, and that he ﷺ met with the Prophets on the night of his journey, in Jerusalem and in the Heavens.
>
> He saw Mūsā standing and praying in his grave. And, he ﷺ informed us that he returns the greeting of peace to everyone that greets him. There are many other such evidences that bring about sure knowledge that the death of the Prophets only means that they are hidden from us, such that we do not perceive them, even though they are existing and alive. That is the same as the state of the Angels. They are existing and alive, though none of our species sees them, except someone that Allah elects for *karāmāt*.

Abū Yaʿlā narrated in his *Musnad* and al-Bayhaqī, in *Kitāb Hayāt al-Anbiyā'*, from Anas, that the Prophet ﷺ said, 'The Prophets are not left in their graves after forty days. Rather, they pray before Allah (ta ʿālā) until the trumpet is blown.' And Sufyān al-Thawrī narrated, in his *Jāmiʿ*, 'One of our Sheikhs said that Saʿīd ibn Musayyab said, "No Prophet remains in his grave more than forty nights without being elevated."' Al-Bayhaqī said, "According to this, they are like all other living beings. They will be wherever Allah (*ta ʿālā*) places them."

ʿAbd al-Razzāq narrated in his *Muṣannif* from al-Thawri, on the authority of Abū al-Miqdām, that Saʿīd ibn Musayyab said, 'No Prophet remains in the earth more than forty days.' Abū Miqdām is Thābit ibn Hurmuz, the Sheikh of Ṣaliḥ.

Ibn Ḥibbān, al-Ṭabarānī in his *Kabīr,* and Abū Naʿīm in *al-Ḥilyah* narrate that Anas said, 'The Messenger of Allah ﷺ said, "No Prophet dies and remains in his grave, except forty mornings."' Imam al-Haramayn said, in *al-Nihāyah*, and al-Rafiʿī in *al-Sharḥ*, that it has been narrated that the Prophet ﷺ said, 'I am more noble to Allah than that He should leave me in my grave after three [days].' Imam al-Haramayn added that, in another narration, he said, '... more than two [days] ...' Abū al-Ḥasan ibn al-Zāghūnī al-Ḥanbalī mentioned that one of his books has the narration that Allah will not leave any Prophet in his grave more than half a day.

Imam Badr al-Dīn ibn al-Ṣāhib said, in his *Tadhkirah*:

Chapter: On His ﷺ Life in the Barzakh After His Death

> This has been explicitly stated and alluded to by the Lawgiver. And it has also been intimated in the Qur'an: *'Do not deem those who are killed in the way of Allah to be dead. Rather, they are living in the Presence of their Lord and provided for.'* (*Āl ʿImrān* 3: 169). The state mentioned [in the verse] is life after death in the Barzakh. It is attained by the unique souls among the martyrs of this nation. Their state is greater and superior to those who have this degree, especially in the Barzakh. However, there is no one in this Ummah whose degree is greater than that of the Prophet ﷺ. Rather, they only attained this degree due to their purification and dedication to the religion. Also, they only became deserving of that degree through martyrdom. And, martyrdom was attained by the Prophet ﷺ in the most complete manner.
>
> The Prophet ﷺ also said, 'I passed by Mūsā on the night I was caused to journey near the red dune. He was standing and praying in his grave.' This hadith confirms explicitly the

life of Mūsā. For, he described him as praying and standing and those are not descriptions of the spirit. Only the body can be described as such. In fact, his specification of the grave is evidence of this. For, if the one being described were a spirit, there would be no need for specifying the grave. There is no one who would say that the spirits of the Prophets are imprisoned in their graves along with their bodies, while the spirits of the martyrs and believers are in Paradise.

And there is the hadith of Ibn ʿAbbās [in which he said]:

> We travelled with the Messenger of Allah ﷺ between Makkah and Madinah. We passed a valley and he said, 'What valley is this?' It was replied, Wādī al-Azraq. He said, 'It is as if I am looking at Mūsā passing by this valley, placing his two fingers in his ears, crying to Allah while reciting *talbiyah*'.[2] Then, we travelled until we came to a mountain pass. He said, 'It is as if I am looking at Yunus passing through this mountain pass, riding a red she-camel and wearing a wool cloak, reciting the *talbiyah*.' At that point, he was asked how he could mention their Hajj and *talbiyah*, when they had passed on and are in the next abode and that abode is not the abode of works. He answered that the martyrs are alive with their Lord and provided for.

Thus, it is not farfetched that they should perform Hajj, pray and draw near [to Allah] by any way they are able. And even if they are in the Hereafter, they are also in this world which is the abode of acts, until its appointed term has elapsed. It will be followed by the Hereafter, which is the abode of recompense, in which works will be cut off.

These are the words of Qāḍī ʿIyaḍ. And if Qāḍī ʿIyaḍ is saying that they perform Hajj with their bodies and leave their graves, how can anyone deny the departure of the Prophet ﷺ from his grave, by alleging that if the Prophet ﷺ performs Hajj or prays with his body in the Heaven, then he is not buried in his grave?

2 Reciting '*Labbayk Allāhumma labbayk...*'

From the sum total of these texts and hadiths we can conclude that the Prophet ﷺ is alive with his body and spirit, and that he can affect the world. And, he goes wherever he wishes in the regions of the Earth and in the Hidden Kingdom. He is in the same form as he was before he passed away. None of it was changed. However, he is hidden from the physical eyes just as the Angels have been hidden, despite the fact that their bodies are alive. But, whenever Allah wills to lift the veils from the person whom He wills to honour with his vision, that person will see him in the form in which he is existing. There is no impediment to that. Nor is there any occasion to specify that it be a vision of his likeness.

The **third** important point is that it was asked, 'How can a number of people who are distant from one another see him at the same time?' It was recited:

> Just as the sun is in the middle of the sky, while its light,
> Covers many lands in the East and the West.

In the *Manāqib* of Sheikh Tāj al-Dīn Ibn ʿAta' Allāh, one of his students relates:

> I performed Hajj. When I was performing *ṭawāf*, I saw Sheikh Tāj al-Dīn performing *ṭawāf*. I intended to greet him when he finished, however when he finished his *ṭawāf*, I went towards him but could not find him. Then I saw him the same way on ʿArafah and in all of the different stages. When I returned to Cairo, I asked about the Sheikh. I was told he was in a good state. I asked if he had travelled and they responded that he hadn't. So, I went to the Sheikh and greeted him. He said to me, 'Who did you see?' I responded, 'My Master! I saw you.' He said, 'O, so-and-so! The man of grand Sainthood fills the entire creation. If the Quṭb were called to from a hole, he would answer.'

If the Quṭb fills the creation, then the Master of Messengers ﷺ does so in a greater way. And we have already mentioned that Sheikh Abū al- ʿAbbās al-Tanjī said, 'And behold, the heaven and earth, the Throne and the Footstool, were all filled with the Messenger of Allah ﷺ.'

The **fourth** important point is that someone may allege that such a vision would affirm companionship for the one who sees him. The response is that this is not necessarily true. If we were to say that what is seen is a semblance of him, then companionship is not established because companionship is only established by seeing his noble being in body and spirit. And, if we were to say that what is seen is his being, another requirement for companionship is that one see him while he is in the physical world. But this vision happened in the hidden world, a vision that does not establish companionship. This is also supported by the hadiths that were narrated that his entire community was presented to him. He saw them and they saw him. But that did not affirm companionship for all of them because it was a vision in the hidden world, which does not indicate companionship.

Conclusion

Aḥmad narrated in his *Musnad,* and al-Kharā'iṭī in *Makārim al-Akhlāq,* by way of Abū al-ʿĀliyah, that a man from the Anṣār said:

> I left my family seeking the Prophet ﷺ. Behold, he was standing with a man who was facing him. I figured that they were doing something important. The Messenger of Allah ﷺ stood for so long until I became upset with [the man] from standing for so long. When the person went away, I said, 'O, Messenger of Allah! That man stood with you for so long that I became upset with him because of standing for so long.' He said, 'Did you actually see him?' I said, 'Yes.' He said, 'Do you know who he was?' I said, 'No'. He said, 'That was Jibrīl. He kept counselling me regarding my neighbour until I believed he would make him my heir.' Then he said, 'If you had greeted him, he would have returned your greeting.'

Abū Mūsā al-Madīnī narrated in *al-Maʿrifah* that Tamīm ibn Salamah said, 'While I was with the Prophet ﷺ, a man went away from him. I looked at him as he was walking away, wearing a turban which he had hung behind his back. I said, 'O, Messenger of Allah! Who is that?' He said, 'That is Jibrīl.'

Aḥmad and al-Ṭabarānī narrated, and al-Bayhaqī in *al-Dalā'il,* that Ḥārithah ibn al-Nuʿmān said, 'I passed by the Messenger of Allah ﷺ and with him was Jibrīl. So, I greeted him. When we returned and the Prophet ﷺ had left him, he said, 'Did you see the man that was with me?' I said, 'Yes'. He said, 'That was Jibrīl and he returned your greeting.'

Ibn Saʿd narrated that Ḥārithah said, 'I saw Jibrīl two times in my life.'

Aḥmad and al-Bayhaqī narrated that Ibn ʿAbbās said:

> My father and I were with the Messenger of Allah ﷺ. There was a man with him speaking to him privately. So, he was not paying attention to my father. So, we exited, and he said to me, 'O, my son! Do you see my nephew ignoring me?' I said to him, 'My father! There was a man with him speaking to him privately.' So, he returned and said, 'O, Messenger of Allah! I said to ʿAbdullāh such and such a thing. And he said that there was a man with you speaking to you privately. Was there anyone with you?' He said, 'Did you really see him, O, ʿAbdullāh?' I said, 'Yes.' He said, 'That was Jibrīl. He was the one that distracted me from you.'

Ibn Saʿd narrated that Ibn ʿAbbās said, 'I saw Jibrīl twice.'

Al-Bayhaqī narrated that Ibn ʿAbbās said:

> The Messenger of Allah ﷺ visited a man from the Anṣār. But when he came near to his home, he heard him speaking within. When he entered, he didn't see anyone. So, the Messenger of Allah ﷺ asked him, 'With whom were you speaking?' He responded, 'A man came to me. Except for you, I have not seen anyone who sat more nobly or spoke more beautifully.' He said, 'That was Jibrīl. There are among you men that if one of them were to swear by Allah, Allah would make good on his oath'

Abū Bakr ibn Abī Dawūd narrated in *Kitāb al-Maṣa'if* that Jaʿfar said, Abu Bakr used to hear the private conversations that Jibrīl had with the Prophet ﷺ.'

Muḥammad ibn Naṣr al-Marūzī narrated in his *Kitāb al-Ṣalāh* on the authority of Hudhayfah ibn al-Yamān, that the latter came to the Prophet ﷺ and said to him, 'While I was praying, I heard someone speaking to me saying, "O, Allah! To You belongs all praise; to You belongs the dominion entirely. In Your hand is all good. And to You returns the affair in its entirety, whether known or done in secret. You are worthy that You should be praised. Indeed, You have power over all things. O, Allah! Forgive me all my past sins. Protect me in that which remains of my life. And provide me with good works by which You will be satisfied with me."' The Prophet ﷺ said, 'He was teaching you how to praise your Lord.'

Muḥammad ibn Naṣr narrated that Abū Hurayrah said, 'While I was praying, I heard someone saying, "O, Allah! To You belongs all praise…"'

And he mentioned the rest of the above hadith.

Ibn Abī al-Dunyā narrated in his *Kitāb al-Dhikr* that Anas ibn Mālik said, 'Ubayy ibn Kaʿb said, "I will enter the Masjid, pray and praise Allah with a praise by which no one else has praised Him." After he finished praying and sat to praise Allah and extol Him, he heard a loud voice behind him saying:

> O, Allah! to you belongs all praise. To You belongs the dominion entirely. In Your hands is all good. To You returns the entire affair, what is known of it and what is secret. To You belongs all praise. Indeed, You have power over all things. Forgive me my past sins. And protect me in that which remains of my life. And provide me with pure works by which You will be satisfied with me. And accept my repentance.

So, he came to the Messenger of Allah ﷺ and told him that. He said, "That was Jibrīl."'

Al-Ṭabarānī and al-Bayhaqī narrated that Muḥammad ibn Salamah said, 'I passed by the Messenger of Allah ﷺ while he was placing his cheek on the check of someone. So, I didn't greet him. When I returned, he said to me, "Why did you not greet me?" I said, "O, Messenger of Allah! I saw you do something with someone that I have not seen you do with anyone else. So, I hated to interrupt your conversation. But who was it, O, Messenger of Allah?" He said, "It was Jibrīl."'

Al-Ḥākim narrated that ʿĀ'ishah said, 'I saw Jibrīl standing in this room of mine and the Messenger of Allah ﷺ was speaking to him privately. I said, "O, Messenger of Allah! Who is that?" He said, "Who did he seem like to you?" I said, "Daḥyah." He said, "You saw Jibrīl."'

Al-Bayhaqī narrated that Ḥudhayfah said:

> The Messenger of Allah ﷺ left and I followed him. And he met someone and said to me, 'O, Ḥudhayfah! Did you see the person who met with me?' I said, 'Yes'. He said, 'That was one of the Angels. He had never descended to the Earth. He asked permission of his Lord and greeted me. He gave me glad tidings that Hasan and Husayn are the two leaders of the youth of Paradise, and that Fatimah is the leader of the women of Paradise.'

It has been narrated by a number of reliable sources, namely Aḥmad; al-Bukhārī in a *muʿallaq* narration; Muslim; al-Nasā'ī; Abū Naʿīm; and al-Bayhaqī, the latter two in *Dalā'il al-Nubuwwah*, on the authority of Asyad bin Haḍīr, that while he was reading surah al-Baqarah at night with his horse tied near him, his horse began to wander. He was quiet and the horse became tranquil. He raised his head to the sky and there was what seemed to be a cloud filled with lights that was rising towards the sky, until he could no longer see it. When he woke, he related that to the Messenger of Allah ﷺ. He said, 'Those were Angels that descended to hear your voice. If you had continued to recite, the morning would have come, and people would have seen them. They would not have been hidden from them.'

Al-Wāqidī and Ibn ʿAsākir narrated that ʿAbd al-Raḥmān ibn ʿAwf said, 'On the day of Badr, I saw two men. One of them was on the right side of the Prophet ﷺ. The other was on his left side. They were fighting viciously. There was a third behind him and a fourth in front of him.'

Isḥāq ibn Rāhawayhi narrated in his *Musnad*, Ibn Jarīr in his *tafsīr*, and both Abū Naʿīm and al-Bayhaqī in their respective works *Dalā'il al-Nubuwwah* that Abū Asyad al-Sāʿidī (*raḍiyallāhu ʿanhu*) said, after he had become blind, 'If I had been with you at Badr at this time, I would have informed you of the mountain pass from the direction of which the Angels came. I have no doubt about it, nor do I dispute regarding it.'

Al-Bayhaqī narrated that Abū Burdah ibn Niyār said,

> On the Day of Badr, I brought three heads and placed them before the Prophet ﷺ. I said, 'O, Messenger of Allah! As for the two heads, I killed them both. As for the third, I saw a tall white man strike him. So, I took his head.' The Messenger of Allah ﷺ said, 'That is so-and-so from the Angels.'

Al-Bayhaqī narrated that Ibn ʿAbbās said, 'The Angels were taking the forms of people who people recognized and encouraging them. I came near to them and I heard them saying, "If they are spurred on by our encouragement, they [their enemies] won't be anything." And that is His words (*ta ʿālā*): "*When your Lord inspired the Angels: I am with you. So, encourage the believers.*"' (*al-Anfāl* 8: 12)

Aḥmad, Ibn Saʿd, Ibn Jarīr, and Abū Naʿīm, the latter in *Dalā'il al-Nubuwwah,* narrated that Ibn ʿAbbās said:

> The person who captured al-ʿAbbās was Abū al-Yusr Kaʿb ibn ʿAmr. Abū al-Yusr was a small man, while al-ʿAbbās was a large, tall man. The Messenger of Allah ﷺ said, 'O, Abū Yusr! How did you capture al-ʿAbbās?' He said, 'O, Messenger of Allah! A man who I had not seen before, or since, helped me against him. He looked such-and-such a way.' The Messenger of Allah ﷺ said, 'A noble Angel helped you.'

Ibn Saʿd and al-Bayhaqī narrated on the authority of ʿAmmar ibn Abī ʿAmmar that Ḥamza ibn ʿAbd al-Muṭṭalib said, 'O, Messenger of Allah! Show me Jibrīl in his original form.' He said to him, 'Sit'. So, he sat and Jibrīl descended upon a piece of wood that was on the Kaʿbah. The Prophet ﷺ said, 'Look up.' And he saw his two feet as blue-green as the sea.

Ibn Abī al-Dunyā narrates in his *Kitāb al-Qubūr,* and al-Ṭabarānī in his *Awsaṭ,* that Ibn ʿUmar said:

> While I was a captive in the shrubs of Badr, a man came out from a hole. He had chains on his neck. He said, 'O, ʿAbdullāh! Give me something to drink.' Then another man came out of the same whole. He had a whip in his hand. He said, 'O, ʿAbdullāh! Don't give him anything to drink. He is a disbeliever.' Then, he beat him with the whip until he returned to his hole. I went to the Prophet ﷺ and informed him of that. He said to me, 'Did you really see him?' I said, 'Yes'. He said, 'That was the enemy of Allah, Abū Jahl. And that is his punishment until the Day of Resurrection.'

This is evidence because the man he saw come out after him, with the whip, is the Angel that has been charged with punishing him.

Ibn Abī al-Dunyā, al-Ṭabarānī and Ibn ʿAsākir all narrate, by way of ʿUrwah ibn Ruwaym, on the authority of al-ʿIrbāḍ ibn Sāriyah, the Companion (*raḍiyallāhu ʿanhu*), that he was wishing to die. So he made the supplication, 'O, Allah! I have grown old of age and my bones have become week. So, take me to Yourself.' He said:

> One day, while I was in the Masjid in Damascus and I was praying and supplicating to be taken, a young man appeared before me, a most beautiful person. He had a green adornment on. He said, 'What is this supplication that you are making?'

> I said, 'How should I supplicate?' He said, 'O, Allah! Beautify my works and cause me to reach my appointed term.' I said to him, 'Who are you? May Allah have mercy on you.' He said, 'I am Ratābīl, who removes the sadness from the hearts of the believers.' Then he went away and I no longer saw anyone.

Ibn ʿAsākir narrated in his *Tārīkh* That Saʿīd ibn Sinān said:

> I came to Jerusalem intending to pray. I entered the Masjid and, while I was praying, I heard someone with two wings who had turned to me, murmuring, 'Glory to the One who is perpetual and eternal. Glory to the One who is Living and Self-subsistent. Glory to the Holy King. Glory to the Lord of the Angels and the spirit. Glory to Allah and may He be praised. Glory to the Most Exalted. Blessed and Exalted is He.' Then, another person came murmuring the same thing. Then another one after that one. They were saying it to each other until they filled the Masjid. One of them came close to me and said, 'O, son of Ādam'. I said, 'Yes'. He said, 'Do not fear; they are Angels.'

ADDENDUM

From that which can be added here is that which Abū Dāwūd narrated by way of Abū ʿUmayr ibn Anas, on the authority of some of his uncles among the Anṣār, that ʿAbdullāh ibn Zayd said, 'O, Messenger of Allah! I was between sleep and wakefulness when someone came to me and taught me the *adhān*.' ʿUmar ibn al-Khaṭṭāb had seen the same person before that. However, he hid it for twenty days.

Also, in *Kitāb al-Ṣalāh* by Abū Naʿīm al-Faḍl ibn Dakīn [it is narrated] that ʿAbdullāh ibn Zayd said, 'If it were not for my suspecting myself of being deceived, I would have said that I had not been asleep.'

It has also been narrated in *al-Sunan* of Abū Dāwūd by way of Ibn Abī Layla that a man from the Anṣār came and said:

> O Messenger of Allah! I saw a man as if he had two green robes on. He gave the adhan, then he sat for a time. Then he said something similar to it, except that he added, 'Qad qāmat al-ṣalāh.' If it were not for what people would say, I would say

> that I was awake and not sleeping. The Messenger of Allah ﷺ said, 'Allah has shown you good.'

Sheikh Walī al-Dīn al-ʿIrāqī said, in his Sharḥ Sunan Abū Dāwūd, 'His words "I was between sleep and wakefulness" are problematic, because one is either asleep or awake. So, what he meant was that his sleep was light, close to wakefulness. It is as if he was at an intermediary stage between sleep and wakefulness.'

I say, it is more enlightening to interpret it according to the states that the people of spiritual states experience, where they witness whatever they witness and hear whatever they hear. And the Companions (*raḍiyallāhu ʿanhum*) are the leaders of the people of spiritual states. In addition, a number of hadiths have been narrated regarding Abu Bakr, Umar, and Bilal seeing something similar to the vision of ʿAbdullāh ibn Zayd. Furthermore, both Imam al-Ḥaramayn, in *al-Nihayah*, and al-Ghazālī, in *al-Basīṭ*, mentioned more than ten Companions, all of whom had similar visions. In the hadith in which the Angel called the *adhān*, it was also heard by Umar, Bilal, and Jibrīl. This was narrated by al-Ḥarith ibn Abī Usāmah in his *Musnad*. This is also similar to what Ibn ʿAsākir narrated in his *Tārīkh*, that Muḥammad ibn al-Munkadir said:

> The Messenger of Allah ﷺ entered upon Abu Bakr and saw him very ill. So, he left and entered upon ʿĀ'ishah to inform her of Abu Bakr's plight. At that moment, Abu Bakr sought permission and entered. The Prophet ﷺ was amazed at the swiftness with which Allah returned his wellbeing. So, he said, 'No sooner than you left, I dozed off. Jibrīl (*'alayhi al-salām*) came and looked intensely at me. Then I got up having been alleviated.'

Perhaps that was a spiritual state and not drowsy sleep.

About the Imam Ghazali Institute

Without a doubt, the Islamic tradition is a deep and vast ocean of jewels. As Muslims living in the West, we have found ourselves often playing an important role in recent times: to preserve and protect our inherited tradition while firmly establishing it for generations to come. The uniqueness of the Islamic tradition is one where each successive generation of scholars has received their knowledge from a verifiable chain of transmission. This has bestowed Muslims in every generation with the ability to trace the source. The Imam Ghazali Institute has been conducting Islamic education intensives of varying lengths since 2007 with the goal of reviving love and attachment to the traditional sciences of sacred knowledge.

The IGI Enrichment series aims to introduce English-speaking students around the globe to oft-neglected topics of unique interest. It is our hope that a student will go beyond a simple read of the text and seek out a teacher with whom they can study it with, inshaAllah.

For more information about the Imam Ghazali Institute, please visit www.imamghazali.org

NOTES

NOTES

Printed in Poland
by Amazon Fulfillment
Poland Sp. z o.o., Wrocław

31098348R00036